An Edwardian Christmas

An
Edwardian Christmas

John S. Goodall

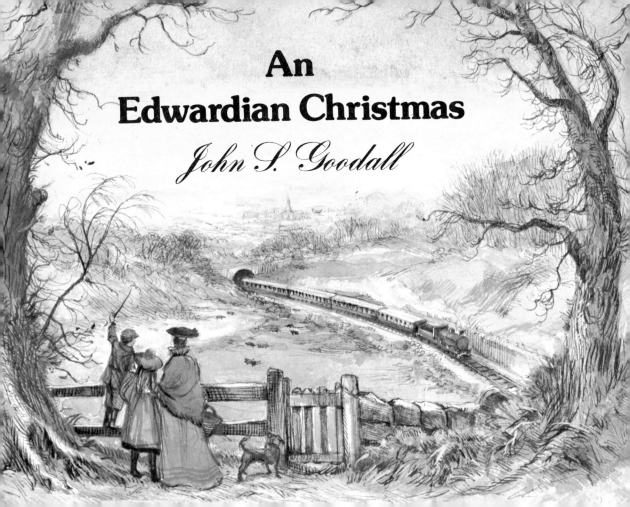

An Edwardian Christmas

BY

John S. Goodall

M

ISBN 0 333 22078 1

First published 1977 by MACMILLAN LONDON LIMITED, *4 Little Essex Street London WC2R 3LF and Basingstoke. Associated companies in New York Dublin Melbourne Johannesburg and Delhi.*

Printed in Great Britain by Sackville Press Billericay Limited

Reprinted 1979

For Margaret,
Sarah and Lavinia,
with love

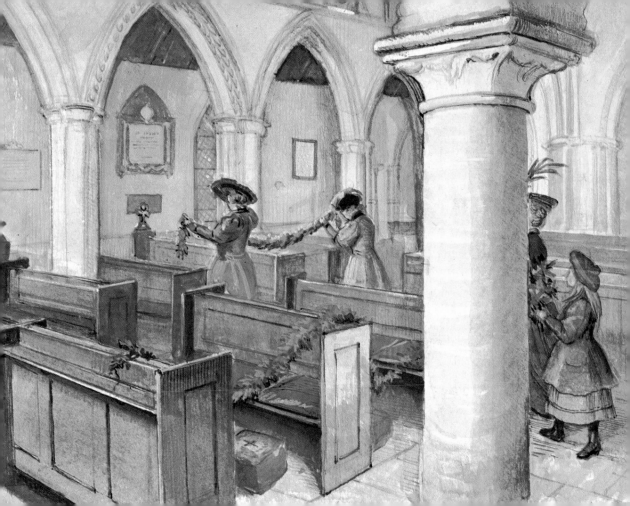

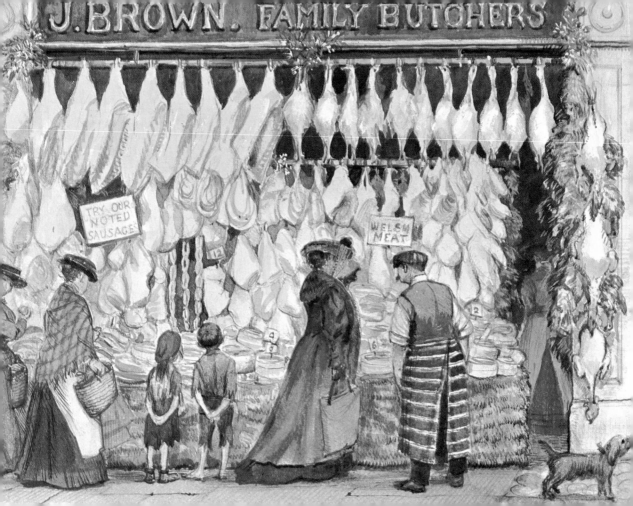

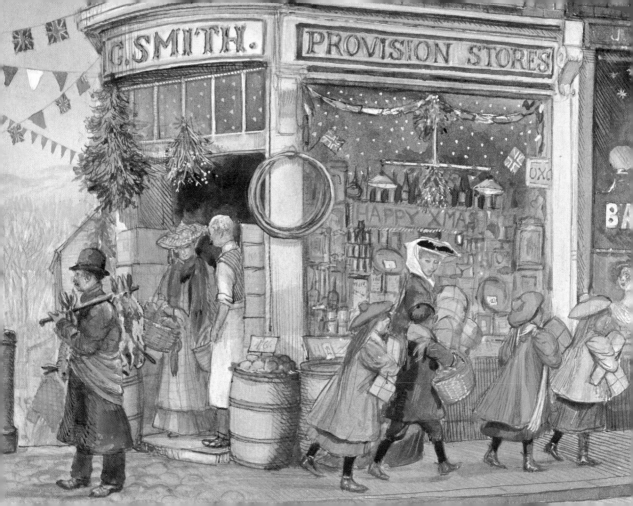

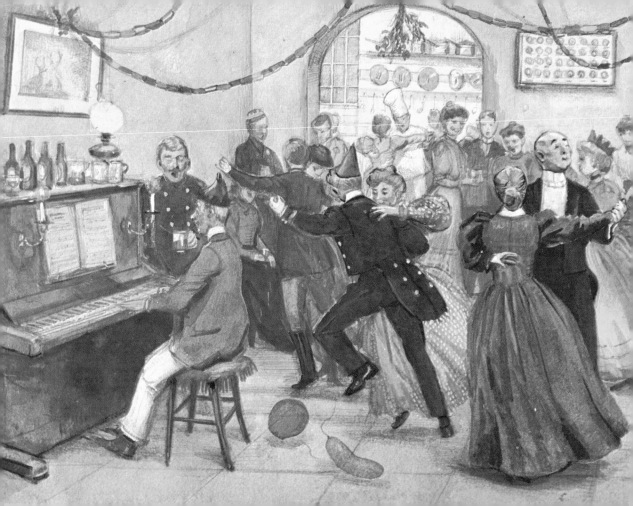

J.S.C